ENVIRONMENTAL DISASTERS

Danube

Cyanide Spill

by Nichol Bryan

WORLD ALMANAC® LIBRARY

Please visit our web site at: www.worldalmanaclibrary.com
For a free color catalog describing World Almanac® Library's list of high-quality books
and multimedia programs, call 1-800-848-2928 (USA) or 1-800-387-3178 (Canada).
World Almanac® Library's fax: (414) 332-3567.

Library of Congress Cataloging-in-Publication Data available upon request from publisher.
Fax (414) 336-0157 for the attention of the Publishing Records Department.

ISBN 0-8368-5505-1 (lib. bdg.)
ISBN 0-8368-5512-4 (softcover)

First published in 2004 by
World Almanac® Library
330 West Olive Street, Suite 100
Milwaukee, WI 53212 USA

Copyright © 2004 by World Almanac® Library.

Produced by Lownik Communication Services
Cover design and page production: Heidi Bittner-Zastrow
Picture researcher: Jean Lownik
World Almanac® Library art direction: Tammy Gruenewald
World Almanac® Library series editor: Carol Ryback

Photo Credits: Cover, Reuters/Goran Tomasevic © Reuters NewMedia Inc./CORBIS; 4, Heidi Bittner-Zastrow; 5, 10, 27, © KOCSIS TIBO/CORBIS SYGMA; 6, 38, Laszlo Balogh REUTERS © Reuters NewMedia Inc./CORBIS; 7, © Jouanneau Thomas/CORBIS SYGMA; 8, © Peter Turnley/CORBIS; 9(b), Image courtesy Scripophily Gallery; 9(t), 23, 26, 30, 33, 35, © AFP/CORBIS; 11, © Royalty-Free/CORBIS; 12, © Barry Lewis/CORBIS; 13, © Hulton-Deutsch Collection/CORBIS; 14, © SETBOUN/CORBIS; 15, © José Manuel Sanchis Calvete/CORBIS; 16, AFP PHOTO/ROBERT GHEMENT © AFP/CORBIS; 17, 36, © Steve Starr/CORBIS; 18, 19, 24, 29, © GREEDY DAVID/CORBIS SYGMA; 20, Radu Sigheti REUTERS © Reuters NewMedia Inc./CORBIS; 21, © Petar Kujundzic REUTERS; 22, 32, AFP PHOTO/SASA STANKOVIC © AFP/CORBIS; 25, © Bettmann/CORBIS; 28, © CORBIS; 31, AFP PHOTO/MILAN PUTNIK © AFP/CORBIS; 39, © James Leynse/CORBIS SYGMA; 40, © VAN HASSELT/CORBIS SYGMA; 41, © Charles Philip/CORBIS; 42, Adam Woolfitt/CORBIS

Printed in the United States of America

1 2 3 4 5 6 7 8 9 07 06 05 04 03

Cover: A worker uses a pitchfork to collect dead fish from the Tisza River after the cyanide spill.

Contents

 # Introduction

"Everything's
Dead"

How do you kill a whole river?

The world found out one rainy winter, the first winter of the new millennium. At a new gold mining facility in Romania, rain waters caused a reservoir to overflow. The reservoir held a deadly mix of heavy metals and cyanide. The rains carried 118 tons (107 tonnes) of cyanide into the Lapus and Somes (pronounced SO mesh) Rivers, and from there into the Tisza (TEE zah) River. Silently, invisibly, the toxic wave moved downstream, wiping out all living creatures as it went.

For twelve awful days, the cyanide plume moved down the Tisza through

The day after the cyanide spill, dead fish are collected from the Tisza River. The fish were killed by the cyanide and heavy metal pollution which spilled into the river at the Baia Mare mine.

Nine days after the spill, dead fish were still being pulled from the Tisza River. Romanian officials denied that any negligence or wrongdoing was to blame for the cyanide spill and insisted the country had responded quickly to the disaster.

Hungary, leaving tons of dead fish rotting on the shore and causing panicked officials to shut off local water supplies. The devastation was unthinkable. Scientists found no life at all in the wake of the poison stream. To make things worse, the lethal plume was headed right for the Danube — one of Europe's most important waterways.

Most experts agree that the toxic spill that started at Baia Mare, Romania, on January 30, 2000, was Europe's worst ecological disaster since the 1986 Chernobyl nuclear catastrophe. Rivers carried the poison through four countries and threatened to damage the environment of a large part of the Danube River Basin. As the plume headed toward the Black Sea,

its deadly effects moved up the food chain — first killing tiny waterborne plants, then killing the fish that ate the plants, as well as larger fish that ate smaller fish, and eventually killing the animals — such as otters, eagles, herons, and bears — that fed on larger fish. Some officials predicted that the recovery time for wildlife living in and around the Tisza River could take as long as ten years.

The disaster had an impact on humans as well. For weeks, volunteers used nets and pitchforks to haul tons of decaying fish out of the water. Thousands of fishermen in economically depressed Eastern Europe were abruptly put out of work. Entire villages that depended on the river for their livelihood faced financial hardship. People worried that even after the cyanide was gone, the waterways might never recover. They also wondered who would be willing to eat fish from waters that had once been poisoned.

The toxic spill riveted the attention of Europe and the entire world. For weeks, people watched television images of workers piling up dead fish and heard dire warnings about the long-term consequences of the disaster. The spill brought a number of issues into sharp focus. Those issues would have a lasting impact on the industrialized world long after the cyanide in the Danube washed away.

The spill raised new questions about pollution and environmental safety in former Soviet Bloc countries. In the 1970s and 1980s, the environmental movement pressured governments in the United States and Western Europe into passing new laws regulating industries that pollute. Factories and mines faced tougher standards which limited the toxicants released into the air, water, and soil. Many environmental activists still fought for stronger regulations for industries in the United States and Western Europe — even though by the year 2000, most industrialized countries had spent the past three decades working to clean up and protect the environment.

In contrast, the countries of the former Soviet Union and the Eastern European nations dominated by the Soviets followed few environmental standards. Communist countries like Romania, Hungary, and Yugoslavia felt they needed to keep up with the industrial production of their capitalist rivals. Government-controlled

"A Total Catastrophe"

"This is a total catastrophe. The Tisza has been killed. Not even bacteria have survived. We will demand an estimation of the damage, and we will demand that the culprits for this tragedy be punished."

— Serbian environmental minister Branislav Blazic

Decaying equipment, lack of safety gear, and run-down buildings — as seen in this Russian factory — are common in former Soviet Bloc countries. For example, the health risks of asbestos exposure are known throughout the world, but Russian factories continue to produce and use asbestos. The Russian government denies any connection between asbestos and health problems.

industries pressured plant managers to increase production and hold down costs. If the managers didn't meet those goals, the communist governments fired and replaced the managers. Plant and mine managers often cut corners on environmental safety or ignored safety rules entirely. The Communists also prevented people from forming groups to protest and push for change. There could be no environmental movement in Eastern Europe as there was in the West.

All that began to change with the collapse of the Soviet Union in 1991. One by one, the countries of the former Soviet Bloc threw off their communist governments and became democracies. Most began to pass environmental laws and form agencies to monitor the safety of the air and water. But a half century of poor economic management left these nations with industries full of outdated equipment that polluted the environment. Little money remained for the repair of decaying buildings.

"Everything's Dead"
"Everything's dead, cyanide destroyed the entire food chain. Fishing was my job. I don't know what I'm going to do now."
— Serbian fisherman Slobodan Krkjes

People wanted clean water and air, but they also needed jobs. The new democracies struggled to balance these needs. For some, the toxic spill in Romania proved that Eastern Europe was still an environmental wasteland.

Like Chernobyl, the Baia Mare cyanide spill also showed that an environmental accident in one country often endangered many other countries. The poisonous plume wound its way through rivers in Romania, Hungary, Yugoslavia, Bulgaria, and Ukraine before reaching the Black Sea. How could a country protect its own waters when those waters first flowed through other nations — each with different environmental laws? Shouldn't everyone on a river system have some input on what is allowed to happen along that river?

The Baia Mare disaster led to a call for increased cooperation among European nations in preventing and responding to environmental accidents.

The toxic spill also focused attention on traditional practices of the mining industry. Most mining companies used cyanide in solution to extract gold, silver, and other precious metals from ore.

Cyanide mining is not a new practice. Cyanide was first used in mining around the turn of the last century. This share of the Yucca Cyanide Mining and Milling Company was issued in 1904.

Fisherman who were abruptly put out of work because of the cyanide spill helped clean the dead fish from the rivers.

The cyanide technique — called cyanide leaching — allowed the companies to recover more of the valuable metals found in lower-grade ore, as well as microscopic amounts of metals from leftover, scrap rock.

In a way, the increased use of cyanide was a response to the environmental movement. Many communities no longer wanted new mines dug near them. Cyanide mining helped companies process more precious metals without digging new mines. But Baia Mare showed the world that the use of cyanide in mining operations posed potential risks of its own. The spill led local anti-mining groups to step up the pressure to close cyanide mining operations in their areas, or to prevent new ones from being licensed.

Cyanide kills, but it doesn't stay lethal very long because it readily combines with other elements. Within weeks, cyanide levels dropped to normal in the rivers as the poison became more and more diluted. However, it will take years to detect the full environmental impact of the toxic metals that were also part of the tailings dam spill.

Slowly, plant and animal life in the Danube River Basin is recovering, but memories of the disaster linger.

Chapter 1

Big
Mine

Germans and Austrians call it the Donau. For Hungarians, it is the Duna. Serbs, Croatians, and Bulgarians say "Dunav." And in Ukraine, it is the Dunay. This river, which English speakers call the Danube, has so many names because it touches so many lives. It is the second-longest river in Europe, stretching 1,776 miles (2,858 kilometers) from its headwaters in Germany's Black Forest to its mouth at the Black Sea. Along the way, it passes through eight nations, all of whom rely on it for transportation, irrigation, and food. About eighty-three million people live in the Danube River Basin.

The Danube River winds through Budapest, Hungary, on its journey to the Black Sea.

The Danube has always held an important place in world history. Barbarian tribes crossed the Danube — which they called the Danubius — to attack the Roman Empire. The Crusaders followed it like a highway in their quest to liberate the Holy Land. The Ottoman Empire used it as a way to spread Islamic power and culture into Eastern Europe. Through the ages, the Danube has been celebrated in poetry and song.

Johann Strauss's "Blue Danube Waltz" ("On the Beautiful Blue Danube") is one of the most familiar pieces of music in Western culture. For Europeans, the Danube is much more than a river. To them, the Danube is what the Mississippi River is to Americans — not just a waterway, but a symbol.

Many rivers feed the Danube. The largest is the Tisza, which begins in Ukraine's Carpathian Mountains and eventually meets the Danube. Along its 600-mile (960-km) journey to the Danube, the Tisza passes through ancient forests, alpine meadows, and lowland marshes. It also passes through sites of heavy industrialization and development.

The Tisza has long been a rich fishery for the five nations along its banks. Sixty-eight different species of fish — including the Black Sea sturgeon, ship sturgeon, Danube salmon, as well as gudgeon (pronounced "GE jen"), loach, bullheads, and minnows — live in the river.

The forests along the Tisza also teem with wildlife that depend on the fish. Birds of prey such as herons and eagles, aquatic mammals such as otters, and fish-eating land animals such as bears all depend on the Tisza. People regard it as a natural treasure, and often refer to it as the "heart and soul" of Hungary, through which the greatest length of the Tisza passes.

"Clear Environmental Improvement"

"Baia Mare has a growing population and urban development with expansion restricted in some areas by the presence of old tailings ponds. . . . Residents are living within 50 meters (164 feet) of highly toxic, potentially chronically leaking, waste sites that cause concern, especially in the dry months. There would be a clear environmental improvement from removing such waste sites."

— From a March 2000 report by the United Nations Environmental Program

Two boys in Baia Mare, Romania, earn money cleaning windshields of cars waiting in line at a filling station.

The large veins of gold and silver in the Baia Mare gold mine ran out in the early 1900s.

But while the Tisza has been celebrated, it has also been exploited. Intensive forestry and agriculture along its banks caused increased erosion and pollution from runoff. Factories and towns on the river contribute to additional pollution.

Farmers and developers drained much of the wetlands in the Tisza River Basin. Wetland loss anywhere causes many problems. Wetlands not only provide habitat for the marsh animals, but also serve as a natural filtration system which helps any body of water clean itself of wastes and sediments. Furthermore, the wetlands function as a reservoir for floodwaters when heavy rains cause the Tisza to overflow its banks. The destruction of many of the wetlands meant floodwaters had nowhere to go but into towns and industrial areas.

Mining is among the most prominent industries where the Tisza River flows through Romania. People have been mining in northern Romania since the days of the Roman Empire. The area is famous for its rich deposits of gold and silver. More recently, miners dug lead, zinc, and manganese from its rocks.

Baia Mare was one of the centers of Romanian mining — even the town's name means "big mine" in Romanian.

The mountain that forms a backdrop for the town of Lens, France, was created from mine tailings. The mines closed down between 1985 and 1990.

By the end of the twentieth century, the big veins of gold and silver ore that made Baia Mare famous ran out. In their place stood huge heaps of mine tailings — piles of crushed and pulverized rock left over from the mining process. Not only were the big mounds ugly, but they also caused problems. As spring rains eroded the piles, the runoff carried toxic, "heavy" metals into the groundwater. (The term "heavy metal" is often used to describe a group of metallic ions that includes mercury, lead, arsenic, and cadmium that enter the environment through pollution. Heavy-metal pollution lasts a long time. These toxic metals can also become part of the food chain and build up in the bodies of animals and humans to cause serious health effects.)

In the dry season, wind carried dust from the mound of tailings into the nearby Baia Mare. Residents believed that the tailings piles were causing illnesses. They asked the Romanian government for help.

Government officials knew they couldn't afford to haul tons of tailings away and store them somewhere. But an Australian mining company, Esmeralda Exploration Limited, thought it had an answer. Esmeralda proposed using a process called cyanide leaching to extract more gold and silver from the tailings. In return, the company agreed to transport the tailings to new, safer storage ponds further away from town.

To the Romanian government, it looked like a win-win situation — more gold and more jobs for the people of Baia Mare, and a cleaner, safer environment once the project was finished. So in 1992, the Romanian government formed a joint company with Esmeralda, called Aurul S. A., which received permits to build a new cyanide-mining facility at Baia Mare.

Mining With Poison

Mining with cyanide is a process that goes back more than a century. The process, called leaching, involves grinding up low-grade ores or tailings and washing them with a cyanide solution. Cyanide combines with the trace amounts of gold and silver in the scrap ore, dissolving them into a solution. Zinc dust added to that solution turns the precious metals back into a solid form that can be sold. This frees up the cyanide, making it available for more leaching.

Cyanide leaching revolutionized the mining industry. The process meant that bodies of low-grade ore with very small amounts of precious metals could yield new sources of wealth. Cyanide leaching also gave mining companies a profit incentive (a way to make even more money) if they processed and restored old piles of tailings that might otherwise threaten the environment. Mining companies all over the globe use cyanide. The process requires huge quantities of water, so these mining facilities are typically located near lakes and rivers.

Residents of Baia Mare welcomed the Aurul project. Construction of the facility held the promise of two hundred much-needed jobs. For the ten years it was expected to be in operation, the facility would employ another one hundred fifty people. The project was not only a boon to Baia Mare, but also to the entire country of Romania.

When completed, the Aurul facility would generate 1.6 tons (1.45 tonnes) of gold and 9 tons (8 tonnes) of silver a year. As part owner of Aurul, the Romanian government shared in millions of dollars in profits.

Best of all, the facility was designed to be one of the most modern in all of Eastern Europe. Its new tailings pond was considered a major

This is cyanide in its natural state. Cyanide in this solid form is stable. When dissolved in water, cyanide becomes extremely toxic.

A Deadly Teaspoon

"The hard-rock mining industry has derived big profits from cyanide. This toxic chemical has made it possible for mining companies to mine low-grade ore bodies for microscopic flecks of gold and silver, and still turn a profit. The use of cyanide in mining, however, is becoming more and more controversial. . . . Cyanide is a toxic chemical — one teaspoon of two percent cyanide solution can cause death in humans. And in recent years, a string of cyanide-related mine accidents has added to community fears and concerns."

— Stephen D'Esposito,
Mineral Policy Center, 1998

The Aurul S. A. gold mining facility in Baia Mare was jointly owned by the Romanian government and Esmeralda Exploration Limited, an Australian company.

environmental improvement. Located 4 miles (6.4 km) downstream from Baia Mare and covering 230 acres (93 ha), the massive pond was lined with plastic to prevent leakage. Special drains placed around it collected any fluid that might seep out. The pond was designed to make certain that all water used in the process was completely recycled and never released into the environment.

Questions About Cyanide

Even as construction on the Aurul project was proceeding, cyanide mining was coming under increasing attack from environmental groups around the world. They protested that cyanide is one of the most toxic compounds known to science. Mines use thousands of pounds of deadly cyanide in their leaching process. Even though Aurul's plan called for recycling the water used for leaching, the tailings would still contain some cyanide. The leaching process also produced heavy metals such as copper, arsenic, lead, and mercury. Environmentalists felt that no containment system was foolproof enough to eliminate the risk of catastrophic leaks.

Critics pointed to accidents like the Zortman, Montana, spill in 1982 — when 52,000 gallons (196,800 liters) of cyanide solution poisoned the drinking water for the entire town — and a 1992 spill at the Summitville mine in Colorado, which contaminated 17 miles (27 km) of the nearby Alamosa River. Environmentalists could name dozens of such accidents where dams holding back tailings ponds failed, poisoning waters, contaminating farmland, and destroying homes and villages.

In fact, since the 1970s, tailings dams' failures happened at the rate of almost two each year. Concerned

"Zero Discharge"
"After removal of the precious metals, the tailings will be redeposited in a plastic lined dam which will provide a totally closed water circuit with zero discharge to the surrounding environment."

— From a 1999 description of the Baia Mare reprocessing facility prepared by Aurul

groups tried to shut down local mines and to prevent new mines from getting the necessary permits for operation.

Officials in Romania were cautious but determined to proceed with the Baia Mare project. Local authorities required Esmeralda to complete an environmental impact assessment before approving construction.

In all, Aurul received fifteen permits for the plant, including approvals from local water and mineral-resource authorities.

When the facility began producing gold from the old tailings in April 1999, everyone involved in the project celebrated. They had a safe, profitable, job-producing new mining operation that processed its toxic tailings as well. It looked as if good times were finally back for Baia Mare.

But the good times lasted just eight months before disaster struck.

Mines using cyanide for ore extraction are found across the world. The Cresson Gold Mine, a strip mine located in a historic gold district near Victor, Colorado, is controversial because of its size and its use of cyanide leach pits to recover gold.

Chapter 2

A Poison
Flood

It seemed as if the rain would never stop.

The winter of 2000 was a wet one for Eastern Europe. In Baia Mare, repeated storms dumped more than 24 inches (61 cm) of snow on the ground. From mid-December 1999 to the end of January 2000, almost 5 inches (13 cm) had fallen. On January 30 alone, more than 1.5 inches (4 cm) of rain fell, melting the snow cover and causing floods in many areas.

Water levels behind Aurul's new tailings dam kept rising. The high-walled pond, which is also called a tailing dam, was designed to grow with use. After the cyanide and zinc treatments removed the valuable

Heavy machinery works on the Baia Mare tailings dam the day after it gave way. The failure of the dam spilled tons of cyanide and heavy metals into the Tisza River.

The sludge from the Baia Mare gold mine has a toxic, liquid core that contains cyanide as well as heavy metals.

metals, the remaining mixture of ground-up tailings and water — called a slurry — was pumped to the dam, where it was sprayed along the walls. The liquid flowed down to the base of the dam so it could be pumped away and reused. The solids settled out and became part of the dam walls. In this way, the dam grew higher as more tailings were pumped into it. Aurul's engineers estimated that by the time all the tailings were processed, the dam walls at Baia Mare would be about 20 feet (6 meters) tall.

By January 2000, the dam had been operating for a few months but the walls were only a few feet high. Weeks of freezing temperatures prevented workers from spraying the slurry that would build the dam walls. Aurul's engineers calculated that even at that low height, the dam would contain normal amounts of precipitation. But the engineers had not foreseen the combination of heavy rain and the meltwater coming from the accumulated snow. To make matters worse, the pond had a thick ice and snow cover that prevented any water already there from evaporating.

Romania Informs the World
"During the night of January 30 to 31, 2000, a dam of S. C. Aurul S. A., a mainly private owned Esmeralda gold mining company based in Baia Mare (North of Romania), overflowed due to heavy raining and sudden melting down of the snow layer and brought into streams and then to the Tisza River an important quantity of cyanide, a toxic waste resulted from the technological process of obtaining gold. The Tisza River is one of the main tributaries of the Danube in the Central Europe."

— From a press release issued by the Romanian government, February 4, 2000

On the night of January 30, the waters finally reached a dangerous level. They rose to the highest, thinnest area of the dam wall. Then, they simply washed through.

Within minutes, the waters carved an 82-foot (25-m) wide, 8-foot (2.5-m) deep gouge, or breach, at one end of the dam. The water, still contaminated with high levels of cyanide, began to flood through the breach. It swamped the land around the dam wall and flowed into nearby drainage ditches.

The ditches led straight to the nearby river.

Around 11:00 P.M., a facility worker noticed the break in the dam wall and ran to tell his superiors. Aurul called the Environmental Protection Agency—Baia Mare and reported that huge amounts of cyanide were escaping from the pond. Then mine workers shut down operations at the entire facility.

Struggling through the night, workers at the Aurul plant tried frantically to stop the deadly flow. Using heavy earth-moving equipment, they scooped up tailings from an old pile and dumped them into the gap. Work went slowly in the pitch darkness. It was difficult to plug a gap that had a constant flow of water coming out of it. By 1:30 A.M., two and a half hours after the breach was discovered, water still gushed out at the rate of 800 gallons (3,000 liters) a minute.

At the same time, workers treated

A local resident siphons potable water from a container in Bozinta Mare, the village nearest the Baia Mare gold mine containment dam.

Two weeks after the spill, a fisherman at the outskirts of Belgrade displays a dead catfish from the Danube River.

the spilled water with sodium hypochloride, a chemical that reacts with cyanide and makes it less toxic. Another nearby mining operation pumped some of the spilled water into its own tailings dam to try to contain the spill. Aurul hoped that all this fast action would keep the accident from becoming a widespread disaster.

Water officials worried that the cyanide would make its way into local wells and into the town's water treatment facility. The next morning they began testing local wells. What they found confirmed their fears — wells showed high levels of cyanide. The officials sounded the general alarm in Baia Mare, warning people not to drink the water until further notice. Then they warned the Hungarian government about the toxic threat to the neighboring country's waterways.

It took Aurul more than two days to finally seal the leak in the tailings dam. By that time, about 26 million gallons (9.8 million meters) of cyanide-tainted water had been released. On February 2, the same day the leak was stopped, thousands of dead fish began floating to the water's surface at Satu Mare, another mining town downstream on the Somes River, which feeds the Tisza and the Danube Rivers. Now there was no stopping the tide of death.

How Cyanide Kills

Free cyanide — cyanide that can react with other elements to create new compounds — is the most deadly form

"The Poisoning of a River"

"Enormous quantities of dead fish are floating on the surface and the spill continues to spread. This is not just an environmental crisis. This is the poisoning of a river. Eighty percent of everything in the river will die. The wave of poison will pass within thirty-six hours, but no one here knows how to cope with the catastrophe."

Atila Juhas, mayor of Senta, Romania

of the poison. The United Nations (UN) later estimated that the waters spilled from the Aurul tailings dam contained anywhere from 50 to 100 tons (45 to 90 tonnes) of cyanide. Much of this cyanide could easily form new compounds with other substances. Many of these new compounds were very poisonous. One of the most deadly compounds formed was hydrogen cyanide.

Hydrogen cyanide gas was one of the poisons used by the Nazi's during the Holocaust in World War II to murder 14 million Jews, Gypsies, people with physical or mental disabilities, and many, many others.

Cyanide enters the body by eating, drinking, or through the lungs. It can also enter the body through the eyes or through cuts and other breaks in the skin. Cyanide exposure causes immediate effects. It prevents body cells from using oxygen. Even if a cyanide victim is breathing, his or her body is actually suffocating. The brain and central nervous system in most fish, birds, and mammals have the greatest need for continuous oxygen. After exposure to high levels of cyanide, people and animals typically become unconscious and die quickly.

Even at levels too low to kill, cyanide causes breathing difficulties, heart pains, vomiting, and headaches.

Fish are a thousand times more sensitive to cyanide than humans. Even a tiny amount of cyanide interferes with a fish's ability to swim. Cyanide-stunned fish cannot escape from predators. In fact, tropical fish hunters sometimes illegally inject cyanide into the waters around coral reefs. This makes the reef fish easier to catch and sell to pet stores. Fish captured this way do not live very long.

But cyanide was not the only

A fisherman Titel, Yugoslavia, holds the carcass of a wild duck killed by the cyanide spill.

toxicant spilled into the waterway at Baia Mare. The sludge also contained heavy metals such as lead, copper, zinc, and manganese. In small amounts, some of these metals are actually beneficial. But these metals tend to build up in body tissues. Long exposure to small amounts of them can reach toxic levels in the body.

These metals also become concentrated as they travel up the food chain. Poisons advance through the food chain from microscopic organisms to humans. It starts with floating, microscopic plants (phytoplankton) and animals (zooplankton). These tiny organisms absorb very tiny amounts of toxicants from polluted water. As insects and small fish feed on thousands of plankton daily, they get a larger dose of poisons. Small fish also feed on insects. Bigger fish that eat smaller fish and get an even larger dose of the toxicant. Finally, predators such as eagles or bears may eat many pounds of the larger fish, getting the biggest toxic dose of all. In this way, small amounts of toxicants in the water become life-threatening doses for larger animals — and humans.

Lead is among the toxic metals that were in the spill. Lead poisoning is the most common environmentally caused illness in children. Long-term lead exposure causes nerve, brain, and

"No Evidence"
"There is no evidence to confirm that the contamination and the damage said to have been caused is as a result of the tailings dam overflow."

— Esmeralda Chairman Brett Montgomery

Phil Evers, manager of the Baia Mare gold mine, talks to reporters at the gates of the mining complex.

kidney damage. Another metal, copper, can cause vomiting, stomach cramps, and headaches, as well as liver and kidney damage. Many of the heavy metals from the spill could kill plants living in the rivers, which affects any animals that depend on the plants.

Three days after the spill, the deadly impact of these toxicants on life in the Somes River was clear to see — and smell. Dead, decaying fish were everywhere.

And the spill moved onward. The Somes flows from Romania into Hungary, where it feeds the Tisza River. The Tisza is a tributary of the Danube.

It was only a matter of time before the cyanide and heavy metals reached the mighty Danube.

 Chapter 3

"In Memoriam
Tisza"

A river of death was heading toward the sea. Water-quality testers in Romania found alarmingly high levels of cyanide in the Somes and Lapus Rivers. Peak cyanide levels measured almost two hundred times the acceptable level.

On February 8, 2000, nine days after the spill, the two thousand people of Bonztna Mare, a Romanian town located on the banks of the Lapus River, discovered that the town's wells were full of cyanide. Poison levels measured sixty times higher than safe standards.

Instead of casting lines, fisherman on the Tisza River collected branches as they waited for the waters to be safe again after the spill.

"Ticking Time Bombs"

"These mines and their waste-disposal reservoirs are ticking time bombs."

— Zoltan Illes, chairman of the Environment Protection Committee in the Hungarian parliament, speaking after the second Romanian mine spill

This South African mine uses water suspension tanks to settle pulverized ore during the cyanide reduction process.

Water purification plants there and downstream shut down to help protect residents from cyanide poisoning.

The plume of cyanide and heavy metals drifted down the Somes River and across the border into Hungary on February 1. Shocked Hungarian officials discovered that the cyanide levels were even higher than the Romanians reported. By the time the plume flowed into the Tisza River four days later, cyanide levels had dropped. But the amount of poison in the water was still one hundred twenty times higher than what was considered safe. Air above the water had a faint, sweet smell — like almonds. It was the telltale smell of cyanide.

As soon as it had received the warning from Romania, Hungary began to prepare to defend itself from the cyanide. Hungarian towns and cities, which rely on the Tisza for drinking water, shut intake valves and issued warnings to residents. Hungarians who lived along the river rushed to stock up on bottled mineral water because their tap water was undrinkable. In Szolnok, a major Hungarian city that draws all of its drinking water from the Tisza, residents were warned to bottle their own tap water before the toxic plume arrived. Hungarians were warned not to eat fish from the Tisza. The government banned fishing in the entire 300-mile (500-km) stretch of the river. Thanks to fast action by Hungarian officials, no humans were poisoned as the cyanide made its twelve-day journey down the Tisza.

Nothing could save the fish. Tons and tons of them floated to the surface, gasping for air as the cyanide destroyed their nervous systems. Salmon, carp, trout, bream — thousands of fish lay rotting on the surface of the Tisza, drifting slowly downstream along with the poison that had killed them.

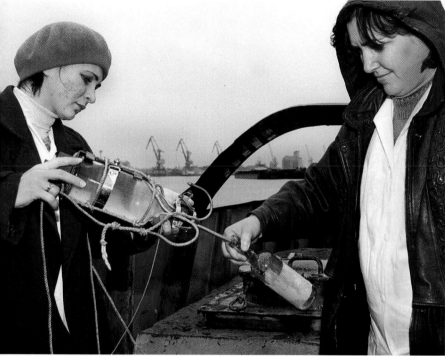

Out-of-work fisherman and other volunteers worked for days to remove dead fish from the water. Working with nets and pitchforks, they hauled the fish into boats, brought them ashore, and buried them in pits. This huge fish-removal effort, occurred along the length of the Tisza. Workers had two goals: Controlling the smell and burying the fish before other animals became poisoned.

"Zero Percent"

"If I said our turnover was zero percent of what we used to sell, I would be overestimating."

— István Orbán, owner of a fish store in Poroszló, Hungary, a fishing village on the Tisza River

For many fish-eating predators, it was already too late. The bodies of dead foxes, eagles and bears were turning up in the woodlands along the Tisza. Some deer and horses that drank from the river and nibbled the grass along its banks died of cyanide poisoning.

Otter in particular suffered disastrous effects from the spill. Tisza River otters spent much of their lives in water which was now toxic to them. The otters were also poisoned by eating fish that had been killed by the cyanide. The Hungary-based Otter Foundation quickly instituted an Otter Ambulance to rescue the endangered creatures. Despite their efforts, the foundation estimated that as many as four hundred otters had disappeared. The loss was especially tragic because conservationists planned to relocate some of the breeding pairs from the Tizsa River area to help replenish vanishing otter populations in other

European countries.

On February 12, the toxic plume entered the what was then called the Federal Republic of Yugoslavia and crossed into the area known as Serbia. By this point, the cyanide levels had dropped — but were still ten times too high. As the poison headed south, Serbian residents faced the same problems as the Hungarians: tons of dead fish to be removed, water systems to be shut down, wildlife to be rescued.

For the Serbs, the disaster came right on the heels of an even bigger problem. The country had been bombed by the United States and its North Atlantic Treaty Organization (NATO) allies who were trying to get the Serbian government to stop its campaign of genocide against ethnic Albanians living in Serbia. The bombing campaign targeted several oil refineries and factories, releasing tons of toxics into the environment. The pollution crisis from the spill stressed Serbia's

It was important to gather the fish that had been killed by the cyanide spill so other animals could not eat them in order to minimize poisoning another link in the food chain.

natural resources even further.

A day after the plume entered Serbia, it joined with the Danube River just north of the country's capital, Belgrade. The tributaries that joined the Tisza helped dilute the cyanide even more. But the level was still toxic and caused some fish kills in the Danube.

The cyanide spill's impact on people's attitudes was even greater than the spill's environmental impact. Here was the Danube, one of Europe's famous rivers, tainted by cyanide from an accident hundreds of miles upstream. Stores selling fish along the lower Danube closed, as did many restaurants that specialized in seafood from the river.

"It's Very Frightening"

"It's very frightening what has happened. People should think about it — not just in Hungary and Romania — but everywhere in the world. People should reflect on this catastrophe and think about how they can prevent doing this sort of damage to nature."

— Julia Kovacs,
a Hungarian who lives on the banks
of the Tisza

The closer the Danube gets to the Black Sea, the slower its waters move. As the river ran along Romania's southern border with Hungary, the cyanide took longer to pass any given point. Once the cyanide plume reached the Danube, another two weeks passed before any poison reached the Black Sea. Fish kills in this stretch were less frequent, but authorities warned residents against drinking the water or eating the fish.

This July 28, 2000, satellite image shows a portion of the river systems affected by the Baia Mare cyanide spill earlier that year.

Villagers in Sasar, a Romanian town near where the accident happened, worried about food poisoning caused by the toxic spill.

One month and 1,200 miles (2,000 km) from Baia Mare, the plume of cyanide that had horrified Eastern Europe finally reached the Black Sea in trace — but still measurable — amounts.

Disaster Strikes Twice

A little more than a week after the cyanide from Baia Mare was dispersed in the waters of the Black Sea, residents along the Tisza and Danube Rivers were stunned to hear of another Romanian mine spill threatening their waters. On March 9, a tailings dam at Baia Borsa, run by the Romanian-owned REMIN mining company, broke under the weight of heavy rain and melting snow. More than 26 million gallons (98 million l) of water contaminated with heavy metals spilled into the Vaser River, which is a tributary of the Tisza.

Downstream, rumors quickly started that the spill also contained cyanide. But the Romanian government denied this, and the spill

A little more than a month after the dam break at Baia Mare, a tailings dam broke at the Baia Borsa coal mine in northern Romania. Dike-keeper Sandor Fazekas takes samples from the Tisza River after the second spill.

did not produce measurable increases of cyanide in the Tisza.

All the same, the countries downstream from Romania — particularly Hungary — were stunned and furious. It seemed as if Romania's mining industry was out of control. How many more of these nightmares would the countries that relied on the Tisza and the Danube have to endure? Hungarian officials angrily demanded that Romania shut down any other mines that posed a hazard to waterways. They handed the Romanian ambassador to Hungary a list of environmental suggestions they wanted Romania to enact immediately. Romania replied that it had the right to make its own decisions about environmental safety. But the Romanian environment minister admitted that there were fifty-five state-owned tailings dams near mines that could produce similar pollution.

The second spill merely added to the rage many Europeans felt toward Romania and toward Esmeralda, its Australian partner in the Aurul mine. People who had lost jobs or had to spend weeks using bottled water demanded an investigation into the accidents. They also demanded that somebody pay for the damages. Along the banks of the Tisza and Danube, people held candlelight vigils that served to protest the disaster while mourning the dead river.

Budapest, the capital of Hungary, was a hotspot of protest. Hungarians were angry at the pollution of the Tisza, which they consider a national treasure. Protesters threw cans of herring through the windows of the Romanian embassy. At a soccer game with Australia, Hungarian fans threw dead fish at the Australian players. Others waved banners that read "In Memoriam Tisza" and "Fish Holocaust."

Children from Novi Knezevac, Yugoslavia, hold placards with slogans protesting against the pollution of the Tisza River during a rally on March 22, 2000. Hundreds of children attended the protest.

The rage grew when officials from Esmeralda tried to deny that there had was a crisis at all. At first, company spokespeople said that reports of dead fish and animals were being "blown out of proportion" by governments and the media. Then Esmeralda officials said that while there may have been some fish kills, there was no evidence that their tailings dam mine spill was the cause of it. The Romanian government, for its part, did not try to explain away tons of dead fish and thousands of fishermen out of work. But it was criticized for being slow to admit the scale of the disaster. As co-owner of Aurul, Romania would share in the cost of any financial compensation that would ultimately be paid.

It looked as if that burden might be huge. Hungarian officials were reporting that nearly all life, including all single-celled plants and animals, had been wiped out in the Tisza. They said that nearly 1,400 tons

(1, 300 tonnes) of fish had been killed by the cyanide. Fish that were the most active in winter, such as the silver carp, were killed in greater numbers. But many protected species, such as the Danube salmon and two types of sturgeon, were also killed.

Less easy to count were the smaller aquatic creatures that lived in the river. It was an important question, because these animals formed the basis of the food chain in the Danube River Basin. They were the food on which larger animals depended. Those that lived along the river's bottom were especially susceptible to pollution's effects. Observers noted many dead clams, snails, and aquatic insects. But it would be impossible to get an accurate count of how many of these animals had actually been killed by the cyanide.

"Blown Out of Proportion"

"No doubt it's a serious incident, but it's been blown out of proportion by the media in all countries. I don't feel that there's been a major ecological disaster."

— Philip Evers, Aurul operations manager

A dead horse is hoisted from the Tisza River three weeks after the cyanide spill. Environmental authorities ordered the highest level of preparedness after the number of dead fish, small game, deer, and horses increased in the contaminated area.

It was also difficult to measure the total impact on birds and animals that lived along the river. In addition to reports of dead livestock, horses, and deer, investigators found the bodies of gulls, eagles, ospreys, herons, and cormorants — birds that rely on fish for food. But the number of dead birds and animals that were found numbered less than one hundred. Some felt that this was because a thorough survey of the wilderness areas around the Tisza and Danube was not made. Others said that the fast removal of dead fish from the river — along with the ability of some animals to sense the presence of cyanide — may have prevented widespread damage to animal populations.

There was no doubting the human toll of the Baia Mare spill, however. Nations along the rivers bore heavy costs for cleaning up the dead fish and providing alternative water supplies for their citizens. Thousands of fishermen were thrown out of work for weeks.

But even after the cyanide had cleared, the economic damage continued. No one wanted to eat fish that might have been from cyanide-tainted waters, so the business of fish shops and restaurants continued to suffer for months. As spring arrived, the mobs of tourists that many towns relied on for income failed to arrive. No one wanted to vacation on a river they had been told was dead. In the area around Hungary's Lake Tisza, a massive waterway created by damming the river, tourism dropped by half.

Hungary's Center for Environmental Studies estimated the total cost of the Baia Mare's spill was nearly $15 million in U.S. dollars. About $6 million of that was caused by losses in the fishing industry, and roughly $8 million was due to loss of tourism revenue. Romanian officials estimated that the total cost of cleanup and reparations for all countries could reach $20 billion U.S. dollars.

When asked who would foot the bill for the loss, citizens, government officials, and even commissioners from the European Union gave the same reply: "The polluter pays."

But who exactly was the polluter? If one was a national government and the other a foreign corporation, how exactly could you make them pay?

In the end, the heavy rains that almost doomed the Tisza and the Danube may actually have helped to save them.

Chapter 4

Signs of Life

Rains and snowmelt in the spring of 2000 caused many of the rivers in the Danube River Basin to overflow their banks. The flood of fresh, clean water helped flush remaining traces of cyanide from the Tisza and Danube, and washed new populations of single-celled animals and plants downstream to replace those that the cyanide killed.

The swollen waters aided the recovery of the surviving fish. Finding little competition, the survivors began to multiply rapidly.

In May, Hungary began to restock the Tisza with fish. Thirty different species were reintroduced into the

The floods in the spring of 2000 may have actually helped dilute the pollution from the two mine spills earlier that year. This bridge normally straddles Hungary's Zagyva River.

Signs warn trespassers of the dangers of cyanide used at the Cresson Gold Mine in Victor, Colorado. The use of cyanide in mining is becoming more controversial in the United States. Many states are considering banning or restricting cyanide mining.

Tisza, including eighty thousand young catfish, which government officials hoped would grow populations lost to cyanide. Also in May, Hungary lifted its total ban on fishing in the Somes and the Tisza. After months of inactivity, local fishermen eagerly went back to work. But catches were down, and people were still suspicious of fish from the once-poisoned waters.

As signs of life returned to the rivers, health officials warned that the danger might not be over. Although the cyanide was gone, heavy metals from the Baia Mare plume were still being found along the Somes, Tisza, and Danube. Unlike cyanide — which doesn't stay in the environment — these toxics killed slowly, becoming more concentrated at each higher level, and causing chronic illnesses as they made their way up the food chain.

Experts from the World Health Organization (WHO) and others warned that researching the effect of the heavy metal spill on the

The Need for Cooperation

"This clearly demonstrates the threat that industrial accidents pose to our environment and the need for countries to work together to improve industrial safety."

— Yves Berthelot, Executive Secretary of the UN Economic Commission for Europe

environment — and on human health — would take years.

Chasing the Polluters

Hungary and Yugoslavia quickly threatened legal action against Aurul's two owners — the country of Romania and the Australian company, Esmeralda. In February, 2000, Hungary filed a suit in Romania to freeze the assets of Aurul for compensation. Both Romania and the Australian firm denied any responsibility for the devastation.

Fearing massive lawsuits, Esmeralda simply declared bankruptcy and put all of its other assets up for sale. The Hungarians angrily claimed that the bankruptcy was just an attempt by the mining firm to avoid paying for the damages, especially because a new Australian/Romanian company — called Transgold — took over operations at Baia Mare. Transgold surrounded the destroyed tailings dam with another dam, claiming this would prevent any further leaks.

No international laws or treaties made a country legally responsible if it released pollution that affected neighboring countries. It was not clear who could be sued or where to file such a suit.

Major Mine Spills Since Baia Mare

Date	Location	Incident
March 10, 2000	Borsa, Romania	Tailings dam failure after heavy rain releases heavy metals into the Vaser River.
September 8, 2000	Aitik mine, Gällivare, Sweden	400 million gallons (1.5 billion l) of contaminated water leaks from a tailings dam.
October 11, 2000	Inez, Martin County, Kentucky, USA	An underground mine beneath a tailings dam collapses, causing the dam to spill 250 million gallons (950, million l) of coal waste into the Big Sandy River.
October 18, 2000	Nandan County, Guangxi Province, China	Tailings dam failure kills fifteen people and destroys one hundred homes.
June 22, 2001	Sebastião das Águas Claras, Nova Lima district, Minas Gerais, Brazil	Tailings from a failed dam wash 4 miles (6.4 km) downstream, killing five mine workers.
August 27 to September 11, 2002	San Marcelino, Zambales, Philippines	Two abandoned tailings dams overflow after heavy rain, spilling tailings into Mapanuepe Lake and causing the evacuation of low-lying villages.

In the spring of 2000, Hungary experienced some of the worst flooding in its history.

On April 27, 2001, the government of Hungary filed a suit in its own courts, seeking about $102 million in U.S. dollars for the damage the spill caused to tourism and the ecosystem, and for the rehabilitation of poisoned areas. The lawsuit named both the country of Romania and Esmeralda's successor, Transgold, as parties to the suit. Lawyers on both sides expected the case to last several years.

The Romanian government filed its own case against Transgold even though Romania was one of the co-owners of the mining operation. In April 2002, a Romanian court ruled that the accident was caused by a "*force majeure*," or an act of nature.

Despite expert testimony that the plant was not built to withstand regional weather conditions, the court ruled that Aurul and Transgold were not responsible for damages. Under Romanian law, the ruling was final and could not be appealed.

Europe Unites

The European Union (EU), an organization of European nations designed to help regulate international commerce, pledged to help clean up the mess and see to it that this kind of accident never happened again. An international commission was set up to investigate the cause of the accident and develop new rules for regulating the mining industry.

The United Nations (UN) also responded to the environmental crisis. It sent scores of environmental experts to the scene to advise local authorities on how to limit damage. The United Nations Environmental Program (UNEP) launched its own investigation into the cause of the accident.

While admitting that the Baia Mare spill was partly the result of freak weather conditions, both investigations discovered serious flaws in the mining operation. They found that the tailings dam had been designed

Kofi Annan, Secretary General of the United Nations at the time of the disaster, called the Tisza River cyanide spill one of the worst pollution accidents in Europe.

"Everything is Safe Here"

"Those who said there'd be no life here for twenty years, shouldn't have said that. Now it will be harder to make the world believe that everything — the water, the fish — is safe here. And everybody is welcome to spend their vacation at this beautiful place."

—Istvan Gyovai, Tisza River fisherman

A group of Australian environmental protesters, referred to as Ferals, demonstrate against the Esmeralda mining company in Australia. The Ferals are afraid a spill similar to the one in Europe will pollute Australia's Clarence River System. The same company is involved in mining operations in both locations.

for expected rainfall levels that were too conservative. Earlier signs of leakage at the dam had been ignored. The investigators also faulted officials at Baia Mare for waiting too long to inform water-quality authorities about the accident. Precious time was wasted as the poison plume started its deadly journey downstream.

Countries in the area began working together to try to head off new mine spills. The nations affected by the Baia Mare spill — Romania, Hungary, Serbia, Bulgaria, and Ukraine — agreed to develop a new joint monitoring system in the Danube River Basin. The system is intended to provide an early warning of any toxic releases that would affect neighboring countries

Hoping to prevent future disasters, the European Union began developing new, more uniform laws controlling mining operations. On June 3, 2003, the EU published a draft of a law regulating the storage of mine wastes. Among other steps, the law would require all mine operators to develop a waste storage and recovery plan to minimize the production of toxic waste and to ensure that wastes cannot be released into the environment.

Mining Under the Microscope

The Baia Mare accident affected people far beyond Europe. Around the world, environmental activists pointed to the disaster as a prime example of the dangers of the use of cyanide in mining. The environmentalists also pointed out the danger in constructing massive tailings dams close to waterways. There was an international call to eliminate cyanide mining. The European Union had already banned cyanide mining for its member states, but Romania was not yet a member. The EU made it clear that if Romania wanted to join the union, it had to close all its cyanide mining facilities.

In the wake of the disaster, Turkey banned the use of cyanide in mining and other countries considered banning it. In the United States, Montana passed a cyanide ban, and similar laws are pending in several other states. Even where cyanide was not outlawed, states passed tougher regulations on cyanide's use in mining operations. Some mining companies responded by adopting new leaching

More Deadly than Cyanide?

"On a long-term basis, the impact of heavy metals on the ecosystem might be larger than the direct impact caused by the cyanide, due to the fact that heavy metals build up in the food chain over time. Therefore it is crucial that a long-term monitoring programme, coordinated between the countries, is carried out."

— World Wildlife Fund, from Ecological Effects of Mining Spills in the Tisza River System in 2000

Examples of heavy metals include lead, mercury, and copper. Heavy metals become more concentrated at each higher level of the food chain as contaminated plants and animals are consumed.

The Danube River rolls past a castle at Passau, Germany.

"The Worst Part of the Disaster"

"A year after the Romanian spill the issue is off the political agenda as officials in Hungary, Romania, and Brussels have tried to forget what happened and what was not done to mitigate the impacts of the spill, assess its impacts, and avoid further ones. Cyanide from Romanian sources recently poisoned the rivers of Moldova. The rivers of the Carpathian Basin are waiting for a similar or more disastrous accident. More cyanide uncertainties are ahead and we did not learn the lessons from the past accident. Probably this is the worst part of the disaster."

— Jozsef Feiler of Friends of the Earth, Hungary

processes that completely destroyed all cyanide after its use. Others looked to other, safer chemicals that could be used to leach valuable metals from low-grade ores.

Despite the alarming experience of the Baia Mare accident and its aftereffects, many countries simply feel powerless to clamp down on cyanide mining. Developing nations in South America, Africa, and Asia rely on mining to provide much-needed foreign currency and jobs.

Governments of these countries entered agreements with international mining companies that left them with little control over the extraction process for precious metals. Tailings

dams that failed in China, Brazil, and the Philippines in the years after the Baia Mare spill caused more death, destruction, and environmental pollution around the world.

Years after the poisoning of the Tisza and the Danube, mining companies across the globe continue to use cyanide in huge quantities. While environmentalists protest and legislators debate, many of the world's waterways remain threatened.

As the global economy shrinks, many people believe that it is more important to have jobs than to debate environmental protection. For the time being at least, they have decided that gold is more precious than water.

Time Line

1890	The cyanide leaching process for gold mining is developed.
1997	Aurul S. A. begins building a tailings extraction facility near Baia Mare, Romania.
1999	Baia Mare facility begins extracting gold.
2000	January 30: Tailings dam bursts, spilling water contaminated with cyanide and heavy metals into the nearby Lapus River.
	February 1: Toxic plume crosses Hungarian border.
	February 2: First large fish kills reported at Satu Mare, Romania.
	February 3: Cyanide enters the Tisza River in Hungary.
	February 12: Plume enters the Danube river from the Tisza in Serbia.
	February 20: Cyanide plume is measured at the Black Sea at the mouth of the Danube.
	March 9: A second mine accident, at Baia Borsa, Romania, deposits more heavy metals into tributaries of the Tisza.
	May 2: Hungary announces the waters of the Tisza are again safe, and begins restocking the river.
	July: Baia Mare mine reopens.
2001	April 27: Hungary sues Aurul S. A. for damages as a result of the Baia Mare spill.
2002	April: Romanian court rules that Aurul S. A. is not liable for damages caused by the mine spill.
2003	June 3: European Union publishes a draft of a new law regulating the storage of mine wastes for all of its member states.

Glossary

assets anything of value owned by a person, company, or organization.

compensation payment.

European Union an organization of European nations charged with setting economic, monetary, and environmental policy for its member states.

force majeure (FORZ mah zher) French for "an act of God." Also a legal term for an unexpected, disruptive, and uncontrolled event that can be used as an excuse not to honor the terms of an agreement.

forint (FOR int) Hungarian money.

genocide (JEN oh side) the systematic attempt by one group to kill all the members of another group, usually because of their race or ethnic background.

heavy metal often refers to toxic metals such as lead, mercury, and arsenic that can accumulate in animals bodies and move up the food chain.

ions charged atoms that can react with other atoms to form new compounds.

leaching the process of removing tiny amounts of valuable metal from scrap ore and tailings by using a reactive solution, such as cyanide.

lethal deadly.

low-grade ore ore that contains scrap rock mixed with valuable minerals.

NATO abbreviation for North Atlantic Treaty Organization, a group of European nations and the United States which ensures the military security of its member states.

phytoplankton microscopic aquatic plants.

reactive a chemical or substance that easily reacts, or forms compounds, with other substances.

slurry a thick, flowing mixture of liquid and solid; a mixture formed from water and mine tailings.

sodium hypochloride a chemical that reacts with cyanide to make it less toxic.

strip mine a type of mine that requires the stripping away of surface layers in order to reach the valuable minerals. Strip mines often consume large areas of land.

Szolnok (JAHL nahk) a city on the banks of the Tisza River in central Hungary.

tailings dam a large, high-walled pond used to store tailings and contaminated water left over from the mining process.

tailings broken or ground up rock left over from the mining process; it may contain small amounts of valuable metals.

Tisza River a European river flowing from the Carpathian Mountains in Ukraine to the Danube in Serbia (Yugoslavia).

toxic poisonous.

toxicant any poisonous substance, sometimes created by humans.

toxin a poison that has biological origins; can cause the production of antibodies in the blood of humans or animals and/or changes in that creature's DNA.

tributary (TRIHB yoo tahr ee) a river or stream that flows into another, larger river.

zooplankton microscopic aquatic animals.

For More Information

Books

The Danube. Rivers of the World (series). C. A. R. Hills (Silver Burdett Press)

Gold. The Elements, Set 2 (series). Sarah Angliss (Benchmark Books)

Water: The Fate of Our Most Precious Resource. (Revised Edition)
Marq de Villiers (McClelland & Stewart)

Water Pollution. Earth's Conditions (series). Andrew Donnelly (Child's World)

World's Worst . . . Chemical Disasters. World's Worst (series).
Rob Alcraft (Heinemann)

Videos

Conserving America: The Rivers. (View Video)

The Element of Doom. (High Plains Films)

Mining for Gold. (Tapeworm)

Mining Seven-Up Pete. (High Plains Films)

Web Sites

Europa: European Commission: Environment
www.europa.eu.int/comm/environment/waste/mining/

RiverNet/European Rivers Network: The Danube River Basin
www.rivernet.org/danube/danube.htm

Romanian Mine Accidents: Environmental Disasters in Central Europe
www.zpok.hu/cyanide/baiamare/

World Wildlife Fund: Danube–Carpathian Programme
**www.panda.org/about_wwf/where_we_work/europe/where/
danube_carpathian/key_threats.cfm**

Index